AF241489

THE RIVER SWEATS
OIL AND TAR
THE BARGES DRIFT
WITH THE TURNING TIDE
RED SAILS
WIDE
TO LEEWARD, SWING ON THE HEAVY SPAR
THE BARGES WASH
DRIFTING LOGS
DOWN GREENWICH REACH
PAST THE ISLE OF DOGS.

FROM THE WASTE LAND   T. S. ELIOT

Published by:
LIVING TIME ® *Press*
Kemp House, 152-160 City Rd
London EC1V 2NX
United Kingdom.

ISBN 978-1-903331-37-8

CIP Data on this book is available from the *British
Library* and the *Washington Library of Congress*.
- Bibliographic Data Records are also available
from *Ingrams, Bowker* and *Nielsen Bookdata.*

email: info@livingtime.co.uk
website: www.livingtime.net
telephone: 0207-1014141
rights: 07930-128892

POESIA NUEVA

Edouard d'Araille

LIVING TIME® Press

Editor's Foreword

The present collection of poetry by Edouard d'Araille includes works from earlier publications (written under his own name and pseudonyms) as well as those commissioned for this new work. It is hoped that the current volume provides a satisfactory cross-section of the range of his content and style, and that it will give pleasure to the widest and most varied audience of readers as possible - I am sure this was the intent of the author, else why write prose or verse at all? You will not find here the expression of one uniform sentiment throughout - no, rather more of a kaleidoscope of feelings and a spectrum of subjects and moments. At some times serious, at others humouristic, sometimes romantic and at others almost mystic - it is hard to describe the work of Edouard d'Araille in a polarized way. For the order and content of this work, I, the publisher, must take responsibility, though there was consultation throughout with the author. Beyond that, the words of the poems must speak for themselves, I can give no introduction.

Series Editor, Living Time ® Press, 2001

DEDICATED TO ALL

POESIA NUEVA

1. POESIA NUEVA

2. THE LOST VERSE

3. GROUND ZERO

4. OUT OF THESE EYES

5. NO/NSENSE

6. IN A SHORT SPACE OF TIME

7. MISCELLANEOUS

A wandering harper, scorn'd and poor,
He begg'd his bread from door to door,
And tuned, to please a peasant's ear,
The harp a king had loved to hear.

Sir Walter Scott

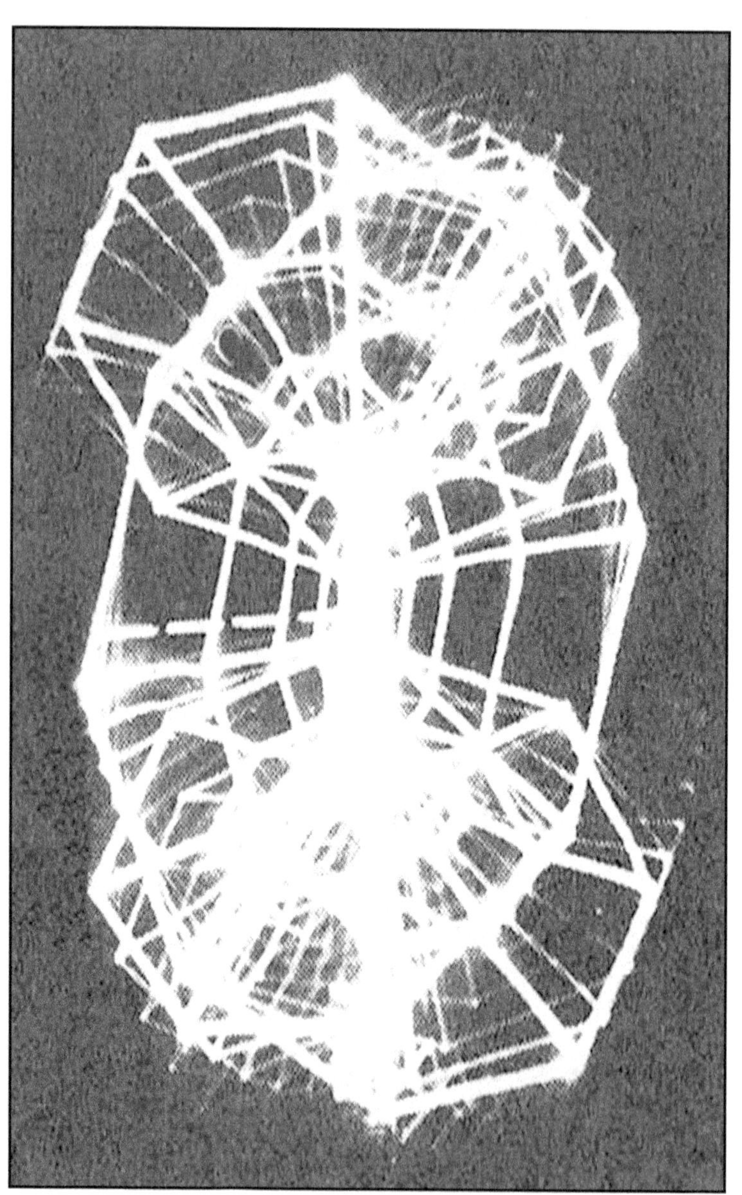

POESIA NUEVA

"The passing of an Age
with a sip of wine - -
I wake in the morning
and life is just fine."

Edouard d'Araille

2001, London

1. POESIA NUEVA

(2001)

Neither the Sun nor Death
can be looked at fixedly
de Rochefoucauld

[A Selection of New Poems
written expressly for this
collection - all during the
year 2001 - Works that
reach out to the future,
delve into the past and
reflect on the present]

Edouard d'Araille

<u>MAN OF STONE</u>

I look for the place that
my yesterday found, -
I want to return
to the stone in
the ground;
I want to read
those words once more
and I want to understand.

I do not remember
exactly where
and
I do not
remember exactly the words

but I know it was somewhere
along this wharf,
beside a bench
and beneath
some branch,
- somewhere
            there
               up ahead...

POESIA NUEVA

There are some seats
and there is a 'gent'
- is *that* the place
before I went ?
The man is standing,
he wears a suit and
a bowler hat - yet
he plays a pipe.

- *No*, as I near
I can see it is not
the stone has
no words
inscribed upon.
and the whistler
whistles his whistle
so badly
I hope the location
is *much* farther on.

I walk and I look
for these words that I want.

The Sun is hidden
behind Big old Ben -
but the waves I still see
as they ring with the bells.

- where is the tablet
of wisdom I seek?
I am sure on this
walkway it was...

- <u>it was!</u>

There is another,
a bench and a tree! -
but no-one is seated,
and no words there ;
cars distant hoot
with impatience,
my own is also
near its end. . .

When will I find
that poem I search?

Then, just as
I lose my belief -
as barges tear scars
in the Sea of Time

- I see a paving
with deep lines etched
beside this couple
who kiss like the French.

POESIA **NUEVA**

I seat myself down on
the next bench along and
I watch as the circus
of life passes by.
Now I have found
my stone, I am ready
to wait till they leave
- till they pass away.

Too many pass
and I do not recall,
even now as I write,
their faces and steps
- who they were -
all I cannot say.

A cyclist rides over
my stone - and
I wish him good luck,
that he does not crash;
children are led by
their mothers
and fathers,
an old man
is smoking his
ancestor's pipe,

pauses,   then exhales.

A drunkard wheels
past me a chair, and
it looks like his wife
but could be his 'ma.

People
of my own country
walk past but
I can't understand
all their words.

The river it changes
from yellow to blue,
the wind, it increases,
the air becomes cold -
the couple recede
their lips and *he*
says "*it is warmer
inside, let us go.*"

I get to my feet
and I take their place
and I sit for a moment
where they had sat. -

there is the paving,
cracked, beside the
the stone from before
- it is just as it was.
I lower myself to
my knees, to the
ground, and I read
the poet's words :

The river sweats
Oil and tar
The barges drift
With the turning tide
Red sails
Wide
To leeward swing on the heavy spa.
The barges wash
Drifting logs
Down Greenwich reach
Past the Isle of Dogs.

Man of Stone,
you are more alive
than a one who lives
and breathes today,

Though dead in the coffin
your petrified words
reach out **as if you spoke**

1888 the year you
were birthed yet you
talk with a voice
just as real as *today*.

Dear TS, did you
sit in this spot
as you watched
the vessels pass?
the river's tide,
is it still the same?
are the waters
unchanged from then?

And I ponder, -
what was it like when
these words were unveiled :

Were you living or dead?

POESIA NUEVA

Were there toasts of
spirit and wine?
Did you drink as the
curtains were drawn aside?
Or was your mouth as
parched as ash?
eyelids already
all covered with dust?

I can find no date
beneath the quote,
know not if you stood
or supine, lay down;
- all that I know is
this old cracked stone
brings alive your verse
and revives my soul -

Thomas Stearns,

you need not return,
you are buried below

*yet **in stone you live.***

Edouard d'Araille

<u>"TEENAGE BANANA"</u>

(BANANOWA MŁODZIEZ)

Don't you remember Jan Kowalski,
the first time he brought
his grapes to school?
and
apples picked from italian trees,
from gardens whose arches
lead down to the sea?

I cannot forget it,
the memory is sharp,
I remember the lunch
that I could not eat :

For where had my slice
of *szynka* gone -
it was not inside the loaf,

had it slipped between
leaves of my exercise book?

had it sailed the seas
to the *States of Sam*?

POESIA NUEVA

All the kids crowded
round *"Jan, the Man"*,
all of his foes had
become his friends,

I watched as they drank
the juice from his carton
 - *Donald Duck* and
'the rest of the gang'

- *he was a popular kid!*

I sat on the wall
of the schoolyard and
looked in my hand - at
yesterday's dumplings
and stale bread

- I might as well eat
my own shoes instead!

*"You should be thankful
for what you have got
and not pine for what
cannot be had!"* - mum said.

Edouard d'Araille

"have you forgotten
the bread that was not
and the length of the
butcher's queue?"

Why couldn't I too
be a "teenage banana",
eat of the food from
the Côte d'Ivoire?

Why do I have to
eat Goulash for supper?
- and Sausage for
Sunday Lunch?

A Saab pulls up and
everyone's friend
is taken away from here,
and as Jan mounts inside
his mother hands him
the holy chalice, the
ark of the covenant,
champagne supreme;

Coca-Cola, - *I dream !*

The Wrath of Hurakan

I

A storm-wind rises up
and Hurakan announces
his Wrath with rains.

Lightning strikes
the steeple,
a bell rings loud

yet time has ceased . . .

The Horses of the Night
are galloping through
the crimson skies,

Bratislava's End is
come, the Crossroads
are bathed in Blood.

II

THE TRAIN LEAPS
OFF THE TRACKS AND
MY BODY FLIES OUT OF
A WINDOW AND INTO A DITCH.

THE NEXT THAT I KNOW I AM
WALKING UP STAIRS AND I
PASS BY THE CROWDS
THAT ARE WALKING DOWN.

THOUSANDS ARE
THERE YET THEIR FACES
ARE BARE, AND I HEAR THEM
SAY, AS THEY PASS:

"*I COULD, BUT ONE HAS
TO BE BRAVE FOR THAT.
I COULD HAVE, -
BUT I DARED NOT.*"

I ASCEND TILL I REACH THE TOP.

III

OUT OF THE MUD ALL
LIVING THINGS CAME
AND INTO THE GROUND
ALL LIFE SHALL STRAY,

SEE THE FACE OF
GOD IN THE ALGAE,
THE ANGEL'S WINGS
ON THE BACK OF A FLY.

*"THE GREATEST SHALL COME
FROM THE HUMBLEST"*

I HEAR THE MASTER SAY
AS HE DID BEFORE.

*"THE HIGHEST
THE LOW SHALL BREED,
THEN ALL WILL COME BACK AGAIN
THE BEGINNING
AND END."*

IV

I AM INSIDE THE CELEBRATION,
WINE AND BREAD IS THERE FOR ALL.

I WATCH THE NEWCOMERS COME,
AND THE LATECOMERS,
THEY, I SEE ARRIVE LATE.

"I AM SORRY, MY FRIEND,
YOU CANNOT COME IN,
THE DOORS ARE ALREADY CLOSED.

NO-ONE CAN FOLLOW YOU
AT THE LAST -
THE FINAL TURNING,
YOU TAKE IT ALONE.

NOW YOU MUST GO
BACK DOWNSTAIRS
AND CONQUER THE ENEMY
- THEN YOU MAY ASCEND."

BEYOND THE RIM

You are seated before the eyes of Shakespeare,
beneath his stern yet impassioned regard, —
and you wish you could write as he himself,
you wish that your pen were as golden as his.

The ancient spirit you wish to contain,
you pray for its reincarnation at night —
"*Step inside my mind so that I may see
and write as you did with such ease*".

And you toss and you turn in your bed,
treasures you seek are beyond your reach.
Trapped in the alleys of dreams, you look
into a mirror but you do not see your Self:

"*I would give my own soul just to write
as he did. Mephisto, where are you hid?
I would give my hand to write with his
quill - I would be his blood upon the nib.*"

Sleeping and waking he finds no peace,
waiting and waiting his wish does not come.

Yet always the eyes of his idol look on,
and they say : '*YOU ARE NOT I, AND CANNOT BE!*'

Day follows day, then months, then years,
Mephisto, for sure, he does not appear;
the poet does not write his 'Lear' but
one day, at last, he sees things clear.

He wakes in the hours of unknown suns
as dawn has not yet pierced the black —
he walks to his desk, and opens a tome
that he has not chosen, it chooses him.

*" WE ARE SUCH STUFF AS DREAMS ARE MADE ON
AND OUR LITTLE LIFE IS ROUNDED WITH A SLEEP."*

— He knows not *if he dreams* and looks up
to discover a smile on the face of his 'God'.

*"Why was I such a fool as to think that
I could steal your soul?! I did not understand
that you live just as much as this fragile I —
AND ALL SHADOWS ARE KILLED BY DEATH!*

*I look at your collar and know it is
that of a Seer - not that of a sham as I;
You hold your head high having glimpsed
with your eyes **beyond the rim** of the Earth.*

Shakespeare, you are not dead!

Your eyes still see with your words;
They *are the Sun that lights our days.*

Shakespeare — I know you live!"

Edouard d'Araille

<u>*Au-Dessus le Pont de Charles*</u>

In the Valley of a Hill and
in the Orchard of the King,
we drink the fruits dry
of their juice and the
trees of their sap.

I close my eyes on
the Hill of King Charles
- and I open my eyes
on Confucius' plain;

the buddha burns in
the light of a candle,
the rays, they emanate
from the flames, -

when will we burn,
will we turn to dust?

- I do not wish for
for the throne.

The Crime

I AM NOT A DANGEROUS SUBVERSIVE,
NOR A VAGRANT OF THE CITY STREETS,
A CONTRAVENER OF THE LAW,
OR CRIMINALLY INSANE,
ALL I DO IS TO SIT
AND PERFORM THE ONLY
CRIME I KNOW HOW TO COMMIT -
TO MAKE YOU SEE WHO YOU ARE,
TO HOLD UP A MIRROR TO MANKIND.

UPANISHAD FOR THE DEPARTED
INTO THE ABYSS OF LIGHT

Sitting below,
before the teacher,
your soul is a state
of the derelict -
the doors are fallen
from their jambs,
windows smashed through
and the roof caved in.

The day is broken,
horizons are gone -
the landscape is painted
in *silence* and *black*.

The time of reconstruction
is gone,
your body cannot be built
again,
all we can pray for your
re-surrection,
return in another life!

POESIA NUEVA

You did not read the words
though they were
just beneath your eye,

You did not hear the warning
though I spoke it
in your ear so many times.

Can you cast a spell
around the fool, and
make them believe -
the **"unreal is true?"**
Or make the wise man
believe the untrue,
that the things that are not,
- **they really are**.

There is no need
to hurry your steps,
they will take you
there in the end.
If not this lifetime,
then maybe the next,
but in any case one day,
some years hence.

Edouard d'Araille

AN AGÈD POET PHOTOGRAPHING HONEYSUCKLE AFTER NOON

One day I watched an agèd poet
photographing after noon -
a honeysuckle near to death
in the light of an ailing sun.

He raised a camera to his eye
- too heavy for his hands -
the shutter clicked although
he could not hear his 2CC.

This is the one I told you of,
the one whose eyes are sealed,
- he who tries to describe in
words what he believes
his lenses have seen.

He puts aside his stick
and leans his back against
the wall of his semi-detached -
his heart is not as strong or as
fast as when he stood before.

POESIA NUEVA

I hear the younger poet ask
(he is standing beside the old):

'What is the Secret of Verse?
How can I compose just like you?'

The elder does not turn his head,
he does not move a single limb,
but speaks in a sullen voice as
if he has said this many times:

"Life is not a Photograph -
The Truth is beyond the Frame

I do not want to disappoint you
- but Moments cannot be caught

YOUNG MAN!

The Secret does not exist, -
do we understand even life!

And then he looked up to the Sky
and recited these words,
(that he said were
not his own):

Edouard d'Araille

IF DEATH BE GOOD,
WHY DO THE GODS NOT DIE?
IF LIFE BE ILL,
WHY DO THE GODS STILL LIVE?

IF LOVE BE NAUGHT,
WHY DO THE GODS STILL LOVE?
IF LOVE BE ALL,
WHAT SHOULD MEN DO BUT LOVE?

and as he recited this verse
I saw the tears well
up in his eyes,

his camera held
still by his side and
the two of them silent now.

Sappho makes
an old man cry -
Shakespeare drives
a young man mad.

[Leeds, 10/06/2001]

2. THE LOST VERSE

(2001)

L'Espérance nourrit une chimère et la vie sécoule *

[A fragment from a dream of death and the beyond, seen from the point of view of a person who can not understand it. Written under the Pseudonym - *S. Amritah*]

* Hope nourishes an illusion and life, like a river, flows on

FROM PART 2:
LAKE DELTA AND BEYOND

Whether or not
I was in a dream or
I sailed on the sea
of my own death,

I did not know
nor care at that point,
I knew that the journey
would take me there.

I sat myself down where
the boatman had sat
and looked across
the vast, vast lake,

I could not see the banks
we had come from nor
could I discern where
the shore was I went,

- but it seemed that
the boat it continued
to follow directions the
captain had given ahead,

the sun was descending
and now it was harder
to see than it had been
when he had been there.

I looked upon the water's
surface - now
it was dull
and it glistened not,

over the edge of the boat
I leant my head
and I gazed
on the skin of the lake.

Before it had seemed like
molten silver,
now it appeared
like pure-white ash -

I touched my fingers to
what had been liquid,
a powdery substance
covered my hands.

I tasted what was
on them and
all I can say is
it tasted like death!

I looked at where I had
disturbed the waters,
the ripples I made
had created a space.

There was an image
right before me -

**there was a face
awaiting me there!**

POESIA NUEVA

I.

The one whom I saw in
this mirror **was me**!
but my eyes
were missing,
they could not see!

I leant my head back
and stood up in
amazement,
I could not believe
what I had just seen . . .

- and then
of a sudden
a gust of wind
blew the mast of
the boat in the back
of my head - it struck
me hard and I fell from
the vessel, my body sank
into the depths of the lake.

Edouard d'Araille

Down and down, deep
and fast I sank,
my feet felt heavy
like stone or like lead.

Above me I looked,
saw a ceiling of white
- the sun and the clouds
were blocked out of sight.

I passed a thousand fishes
and creatures whose
names I had learnt
in no book before.

I passed a forest of trees
and admired the fruit
and the branches
and trunks and leaves.

I opened my mouth but
I did not choke,
- water
filled up my lungs,
replenishing them like air.

I breathed in deep and
continued to sink, it
seemed as if someone
were pulling me down.
I thought that in water
I would feel lighter,
- I felt as if I were
a bar of gold!

Now I was nearing
the base of the lake,
looking down I saw
coral around my feet.
The animals did not
disturb me, behaving
as if I were sleeping,
- as if I were dead.

Down and down
I sank and I sank
till all around me
was cold and black.
I cannot remember
what happened next,
perhaps I slept long
- but then I awoke!

II.

I looked at my body
laid out on a stone
- my clothes, I saw,
were wet no more!

I thought that I woke
within a dream yet
the cave around me
- it seemed quite real.

There above me
stood a figure,
I saw him speak
but I heard him not.

Your body shone bright
like an angel though
I did not recognize
then **which one.**

I got to my feet and
you waved your hand,
you ushered me: "COME,
WE HAVE WAITED TOO LONG!"

III.

*"Hear the Voice of the Bard
Who present, past
and future sees;*

*Whose ears have heard
the Holy Word,
That walked
among the ancient trees"*

Blake,
you take me by the hand,
I realize then the angel
you are,

I read
your words as I sat in the
light of the sun and moon
and stars.

You tell me:
*"Come this way and I will
show you things you have
never seen."*

Edouard d'Araille

You point me
to a hole in the wall of the
cave and you say: "*After
You, dear sir!*"

Through
the doorway of stone I step
and you follow me close
behind,
you tell me:

"*Carry onwards, the land
that we look for is on the
other side.*"

And so we pass
down fiery alleyways,
archways of crystal and
domes of light.

You lead me
into an unknown land like
the one that you promised,
then you said:

"Here beneath
the water's depths,
a place where
is no human breath,
here are
the Halls of Los, the
ageless
corridors of Time,

here, in fact,
time does not stop,
it lives forever
and does not pass.
Here, every
life and combination,
all will be
revealed to you.

Do not be
surprised as you have
walked these
halls of time before –
every thing
you see will seem not
unfamiliar
or strange to you.

IV.

You did not say more
but you led me forth
and took me down
these ancient halls,

you showed me
all that was true, -
you showed me the
dramas old and new.

The future too, you
revealed to me, not
just what has been
but what will be,

I thought you would
show me God himself,
I did not know what
else I would see!

———————————

POESIA NUEVA

I saw Adam
in the garden,
Eve I saw take
from the tree, -

I met Enkidu
in the forest, he
had been killed
by a holy beast.

I saw the cup that
held Borgia's poison,
 saw the chests of
Solomon's gold,

I saw Napoleon
lead his nation and
I saw him die on
Helena's isle.

Achilles jumped the rift
too wide and Faustus
lost his soul divine,

Edouard d'Araille

Tristan loved whom he
should not and Sisyphus
. . . he tried and tried.

I saw my father
take his wife and
I witnessed the birth
of an only child,

I saw myself in
the womb of the earth,
and I saw an infant
grow into a man.

I watched my life
cross a thousand miles,
I saw the beginning
and saw the end.

I saw the last time
the clock had struck
when I did not hear
the hour chime.

I saw men rise and
I saw their demise,
conquests of armies
and millions dead,

I saw a cataclysmic
explosion, the earth
I inhabited gone
up in smoke.

The more that
he showed me
the less it made sense, -
I could not understand.

It seemed to be fraught
with illogic, **unsense** -

*what was the point of
the scenes that I saw?*

Even if that were
the dress rehearsal,
a dream or a fiction, -
was anything **more**?

If the course of all life
has been that in the hall,
then what was the point
of living at all? - - - - -

If anyone told me what
I would have seen there
then I would have said
that they lied and lied,

but now I have seen
the **Wheel of Fortune**
I know how it turns,
I know what is so:

"What is the point of
*a **'House of God'***
if men kill him off
in their hearts?

What is the point of
*a **'love divine'***
when we prostitute life
for sin and wine?

Abraham, Noah, and all of
the Saints, the Prophets,
Dear Jesus and God, -
what is the point of
the human race if
it ends in War and Death?"

V.

*"Do you
not know the unstoppable
onslaught
of age cannot be stopped,
nor can it
be slowed or held back in
its path:*

The advance is absolute!

*I am not God and
I cannot change that
I am an angel -
I am no more,*

*what you would know,
this I cannot answer.
For that you must find
the words on the floor.*

*All I can say is that life
will continue and
I will continue
to walk these halls,*

*EVERYONE CROSSING
THE LAKE OF THE DELTA
CAN FIND ME IF ONLY
THEY SINK BENEATH.*

*YOU TELL ME I TALK
IN RIDDLES, AND THROW
YOU ENIGMAS THAT YOU
CANNOT UNDERSTAND.*

*"EXPLAIN WHAT YOU SAY"
- THEN WHAT WOULD YOU
KNOW THAT YOU HAVE
NOT KNOWN ALL OF
YOUR LIFE, IN FACT?*

*WE ARE SURROUNDED BY
HEAVEN AND HELL,
THE TWO ARE IN ONE,
THEY ARE INTER-COMBINED.*

*IN AN INSTANT WE PASS FROM
THE CELL TO THE GARDEN, -
FROM DESERT OF MANNA
TO FIELDS OF ASH."*

3. GROUND ZERO

(1999/2000)

*whatever a poet writes
with enthusiasm and
a divine inspiration
- is fine*
Democritus

[A Selection of poetry from
a collection composed and
assembled on moving from
the close of the 1990's to
the year 2000. Written under
the pseudonym L. Chronos]

IN THE NIGHT

I wake in the night
and I know
that
the world
that I dream
is as real as that which I see

I walk in the light that I see
and I know
that
I will not
fall down or falter

here all we accomplish
is really gained
and all
that we lose
- is really lost

until we regain it again

Edouard d'Araille

<u>GROUND ZERO</u>

I am walking
yet
I am not walking

I travel the streets
though
I do not move at all

the cigarette ash
     tumbles

   onto

       the

   f
    l
        o
     o
          r

- I do not see it fall

I see people -
you do not see me

I hear voices -
what do you say to me?

*"begin to cease to wonder
we start
from ground zero*

- your time begins now!"

I CROSSED THE SANDED

BORDERLINE

AND SAW TIME WAS NO MORE

<u>Human am I</u>

feelings are buried
within this body -
yet I do not
feel at all

my feet have fallen
by the roadside
I have outrun
- *my soul* -

storm in a crystal,

lightning

inside,

angel

dust

- *I am blown aside*

POESIA NUEVA

I cannot tell you
where I am
nor say
where I
have been

thoughts
unthought
and   words
unresounding

pages unwritten

the canvas blank

*my face is buried
in the gutter*

drunken

drug-dazed

human am I

Edouard d'Araille

<u>T</u>HE <u>S</u>TARLESS <u>D</u>EPTHS

I step
into the
starless depths

garland of night
draped over
my chest

I grow
into the
infinite   spaces

time, are you ready
to meet me now?

you will know me
when you find me

you will expect me
when I have arrived

*I do not
know who you are
- but I do
not want to
hold myself back - **any more***

In Love with Oblivion

52

WHY BE IN LOVE

WITH OBLIVION?

ALL THAT WE HAVE IS TODAY

HERE WE EXIST AND

NOWHERE ELSE

WE WILL NEVER

BE HERE THE SAME

Edouard d'Araille

<u>Time Lost</u>

I lose you

I find you

time is lost

the passage
		way
into the absent past

a stranger to you

I do not know me

my feet walk me
downward
the
unseen path:

> *"love is not free
> 	to you or me*
>
> *- WE DIE -*
>
> ***that** is the cost"*

POET OPIATE

I see you in the mirror

self, are you the self

you seem to be?

I have to become
myself before
I can tell you
who you be

haloic light encircle

my eyes, embraid

me with your

ring of fire

if I lose myself

I may find myself

let me lose myself again!

<u>SWEET AS</u>

55

sweet as
the warmth
of embrous ash,

sweet as
the scents
of memory past,

sweet as
the sound
of morning rain,

sweet as
the glow of
the candle's flame -

what could satisfy more?

sweet as
the touch
of your caress,

sweet as
one more
lychee kiss,

sweet as
sun showers
in my eyes -

sweet as love

untainted

pure

- *YOU SATISFY ALL*

4. OUT OF THESE EYES

(1999)

SI QUIS TOTA DIE CURRENS
PERVENIT AD VESPERAM
*SATIS EST ***
Petrarque

[A Segment from this 'poetic
story' that relates a journey
into a desert of life, fear and
its obstacles, the path of one
seeking answers. Written under
the Pseudonym - *S. Amritah*]

* If a man who wanders all day
arrives toward evening - it is enough

FROM PART 1:
THE DARK CHAMBER

I saw the seer
and
I became what he saw

I hear the talker
and
I become who you are

 I see my face in the mirror
but I do not see myself

all that I see is appearance
- I do not see the rest

the photo I see
it is held in my hands

the words I can hear
- they are on my lips:

Edouard d'Araille

*"out of the pitch
black infinite
I cross the
threshold
into light,
arrows fires
sear into these eyes,
sand showers time
streams over this flesh
whose figure stares out
of the silvery glass,
whose features
are they that I see -
whose raiments of
flesh do I wear today,
whose heart beats
beneath this chest?*

*I do not know why
these eyes are open,
nor of the reason
that I have awoken
- how did something
come of nothing,
where were we all
at dawn's first light?"*

the wheel returns on
its own rotation,
a cycle of time
recommencing again
- spherical harmony
ever unbroken,
destiny paths
repeating

again

*"where do we come from
and where do we go
and for why are we here
and for how is it so*

*- what do I feel
and think and know,
tell me what is for real
and what is for show?"*

I see my face in the mirror
but I do not see myself

all that I see is appearance
- I do not see the rest

Edouard d'Araille

"LA VIDA ES SUEÑO"

the doors of the night
have been opened again
- we slip into a dream

meeting beside a fountain
I ask *'have I met you before,
do I know your name?'*

you answer me not
but lead me aside -
taking me by the hand

through the bakery window
I read your lips
"une baguette s'il vous plaît"
- will we share this bread?

water on charcoals,
eyes filled with steam
- sleepwalking into
a smoke-filled dream

the doors of the night
lead to spaces now distant,
to hours forgotten and
time not yet lived

crossing the border
I know you once more,
tonight and forever
reliving again

cider-filled glasses
of apple bound kisses
- return to my cheeks,
return to my lips

*the doors of the night
have been opened again*

- WE SLIP INTO A DREAM

Edouard d'Araille

FROM THE INTERLUDE:
THE LAKE TONIGHT

*I am within the scene again
in the dream I remember
the night that you left*

*I stand on the shores
of the firewaters -
remove my clothing
and out to you swim*

*light streams
rush past my
feet and my ears,
vistas fluorescent
with milky white tears*

*I CANNOT BELIEVE WHAT I SEE
or rather
I DO NOT WANT TO BELIEVE
WHAT I SEE*

your body floats still
on the lake tonight -
your pale eyes
reflecting
astral
flesh,
cheeks
caressed
by the moon's
own sweet kiss,
your body as cold
as the watery fish

the words that you said
I recall them afresh -
the words you said
before you left:

"love at a distance
is not beyond reach
for no thread of

detachment

can separate us

- the dialogue

may   be   broken

but it is not lost

and when I am dead
for you still I will live
and when voices
are absent
ears will hear -

**what was said
cannot be unsaid**

you do not need to
sleep beside me,
to feel the pulse of
my beating heart
you do not need to
be in my arms -

**with or without me
you'll come to no harm"**

FROM PART 4:
THE STRANGER

it was then that you
approached me
- *YOU* I will
never forget

the moment that
I had forgotten you
came to remind me
of what I had left

you called as I
walked the sands
- *how can I thank*
you who saved me?

you handed me water,
you handed me bread
- as I eat and drink
  to me you said :

Edouard d'Araille

*"I AM SOMA AMRITAH -
I AM THE IMMORTAL DREAM*

*I AM ALL THAT YOU KNOW,
I AM ALL THAT YOU SEEM*

*I AM THE SONG - AND
I ONLY LIVE WITH THE SINGING*

*I AM THE DREAM - AND I ONLY
EXIST IN THE DREAMER'S EYES*

*YOU DO NOT REMEMBER
ME NOW   BUT MY VOICE
YOU HAVE HEARD BEFORE*

*IN THE MORNING
I LEAVE YOU,
AT NIGHT I REJOIN YOU
IN DARKNESS*

*YOU CROSS TO MY
SIDE OF THE MIRROR,
YOU WALK THROUGH THE
FRAME OF THE INFINITE DOOR"*

POESIA NUEVA

And as I sat and ate
I listened
I watched him
he did not move at all

silent for a moment,
head buried deep
within his chest

right hand on
his left shoulder,
left upon his right

- why was he here in
the first place,
*how could he
live in this heat ?*

So when I had finished
the bread in my hand
and lain the gourd
upon the sand

I turned to him
and asked him -

Edouard d'Araille

'Where do you come from
and why are you here?

I recognize your voice,
though I do not know
where I heard it before

I recognize your face,
its features in some way
to me not unknown'

"ARE YOU ASKING ME
WHERE I HAVE COME FROM,
MY VILLAGE OF BIRTH,
THE FATHERLAND?

- THE MAPS HAVE
LONG BEEN BURNT,
THE CALENDARS LOST
- YOU WILL NEVER
BELIEVE WHAT I SAY!

THEY SAID
I WAS THE SHAMAN'S SON,
THAT WHEN I SPOKE - I LIED !

POESIA NUEVA

*The villagers all
resented me,
they said I had to leave*

*And on the **first day**
as I left
this house
unadorned
I turned and said
   - to them...*

*"Beware of Miracles,
Beware you Resurrect!
Doubt is your Death
and Hope - has none
the life you have will
   soon be gone"*

*- I turned away,
return did not -
the words enigmas
they did not want!*

Edouard d'Araille

- LET ME TELL YOU OF THE PAST AND
LET ME SPEAK OF INCARNATION -
I SAW THE MORTAL SIN OF CAIN,
I DRANK AT THE TRANSFIGURATION

I HAVE DONE MY JONAH,
I HAVE CLIMBED MY SINAI,
THE BELLY OF THE WHALE
IT HAS PUKED ME OUT ENTIRE

THE MOUNTAIN I DESCENDED,
TABLETS FALLEN ON THE WAY

I SCALED THE WALLS OF JERICHO,

THEY FELL   I DID NOT DIE

THEY SAID MY SWEAT
WOULD COMFORT TEARS,

THIS BLOOD THE DEAD AWAKEN

WHERE WERE YOU AS I FELL DOWN

- I THOUGHT YOU SAID YOU'D STAY?"

- at this point
   he opened a satchel,
   took out a pouch
   and lit some wood

   *'who do you mean that you are?
   what you say exceeds all sense'*

- he handed me a pipe and said

"PARTAKE OF IT WITH ME,

   THE WHEELS OF THE WORLD

                  WILL STOP

AND THEN YOUR EYES WILL SEE!"

Edouard d'Araille

5. NO/NSENSE

(2000)

*Nowhere is some place
that no-one has gone*

*or somewhere we met
that we have not come*

[Selections from a collection
of poetry which investigates
the borderline between sense
and no/nsense, the real and
the surreal - Included there
under several pseudonyms]

<u>SOY !</u>

Eyes   Mirrors

Within   Beyond

I do not see

I stand here

SOY   I Am

I Live   I Be

<u>Soul Jar</u>

where did I leave my soul?

- was it left in a jar?

where did I forget my body?

- am I still in the car?

I thought I had parted
this land yet I find
that my Self, it
is here once again -

stand still the hours
wait for me still
- and I ask :
is this planet Earth?

I follow the stars
in their paths ... but
I soon lose their tracks
and end up in a bar

I hear that Time
it rides on the back
of a sword held aloft
by a templar knight

"where did I went?"

I ask my friends:

and they say to me :

"far from your seat

beyond this sphere

beyond these doors

and into the storm

of the eye of God"

<u>Unmarried / Unmarred</u>
77

Ishii keeps them smiling

Watanabé makes them cry

Tanaba feels the river flow

Suzuki speaks no lies

<u>Unmarried / Unmarred</u>

A Baby's Dream

a baby
it dreams
of moonlight gone

stars   comets

meteors   sun

it eyes are drowned in
a constellate sky

but it cannot yet
speak of the light within

"*tell us of what
you have seen and dreamed?*"

I do not hear a word

yet sights
that drift through
the circus master's hoop
I know they are the same

Edouard d'Araille

the magician throws
carousels out of his hat
the effect is his final
and greatest and last

a crocodile rides in
a pram as it races
pencil sketches in
the skies unbent

a daffodil flower
cigar in its mouth
- cumulo nimbus -
a cloud of smoke

the snail upon
the rainbow has
left no tracks and
its antlers are burnt
in the rays of the sun

they have both fallen off

an umbrella'd clown
I watch as he
crosses the
tightrope held up by the

hippo   and   bear

rhino   elephant

tortoise and all of the rest

- yet who holds them up?

don't you see what is
coming at us,
the end
is already in sight!

the hymn to the event
is already over -
do you
hear
the slugs and snails kiss?

<u>In The Eye of The Whale</u>

in the eye of the whale
I see my God
he peers
at me
close though
his spirit has fled

I remember before
as I watched
as you
sprayed
the universe
out of the hole in your back

I thought that the ride had
just begun
that the wind
would allow us
to travel for long

where is the edge of
sound and light -
does the universe
end where begins the night?

BALLAD OF THE BROKEN SUN

the light of a broken sun
the song of a fallen son
the shape of life coming
out of an earthen womb

- I was born not long ago
and will not die long hence
the cycle is almost complete
this time I'll leave for once
and evermore ...

I wrote my life on
a canvas of sand but
the words were effaced
by the evening's tide

I saw the crack between
the worlds - oblivion inside

I could not see any more within
- who I had been had gone away

I sought my old self everywhere
I could not even find my clothes

<u>DOG HOTEL</u>

I left You at the Dog Hotel and

I said - I won't be long

three weeks passed

when I came back

- they tell me

She is Gone!

You were

my Beloved

my Chihuahua

Dachsund Labrador

You were my Afghan Buddha

You were my Holy Dog after all!

LIFE IS HARD

LA VIE EST DURE

DAS LEBEN IST SCHWER

ZYCIE JEST TRUDNE

LIFE IS HARD –

they do not

sound the same to me

and I guess they are

not so at all

<u>These Three Things...</u>

these three things
that say *"best before..."*
- hidden within
the outer fridge door

I thought you said
they were already eaten

I thought you said
they had already gone

the pears are turning
but isn't it obvious
they don't know
which way to turn?

the strawberries all
now green
not red
the raspberries
fused into one

the mutton joint
in mildew coat
protecting itself
from the cold and frost

these three things
in the outer fridge door

like them
I don't know
which way to turn

<u>Dear Grandad,</u>

dear, dear grandad,
what did you do?

I want to know
all about your past

I want to know
all that you ever said
- both the wise man
and the fool

when were you born?
and how did you live?
send me a letter and
say when you slipped

"*Je ne regrette rien*" -
can you sing with Piaf?

can you say that you
jumped in the sea without
pausing to think it was wet?

6. IN A SHORT SPACE OF TIME

(1998)

Come, fill the Cup, and in the Fire of Spring
The Winter Garment of Repentance fling :
The Bird of Time has but a little way
To fly - and Lo ! the Bird is on the Wing.
Omar Khayyám of Naishápúr

[Selections from a volume
of verse in which the poet
returns to earth to re-view
the life that he led before -
only work written unde
Pseudonym A. Pathos]

<u>The Fall of The *Arcturian*</u>

is it true we are all of the starborn people
true we were moulded from clay of gold

of the disparate and desperate
and of those who have no home
of the hopeless and the heartless
- of these he has become one

the rats are gnawing at your bones
the air you breathe is not your own
there's damage done
            existing in such penury
this death and dying can do
your soul no good

wise man   fool   *Arcturian*
- *why the fall from grace*
it is not events conspire against you
but you who conspire against yourself

I watch you read the deadly letter
hermes touching you by the hand
the days of radiance   all are over
the tulip wilted   the love   *dead*

you are caught in the grip
of a landslide of shame
and you bury yourself
in a coffin of blame
suckling at the bosom of fate
craving death —- *annihilation*

wise man   fool   ***Arcturian***
a voice is calling in your dream -

"you must still be strong
though the light has no source
and the night has no end
don't give up on love for dead and
don't give up on life quite yet
be done with fear of debt
and lead a life without regret"

wise man   fool   *Arcturian*
why the fall from grace
as you faltered must you rise again

- a phoenix out of the flames

your hazelstick   *is it out of season*
your lavender   *has it burnt its last*
of your own blood don't drain yourself
of your own soil **be not dispossessed**

can you hear the musicianers playing -
sail on Blue Danube
the river will shed no tears
the sea will transpire no fears

hold out your hope to the future
hold out your heart to the wind
bless the days that you are here
for the past is of no concern

time goes by *but where are you going*
hope flies high   then its all over
what is there to fear but fear of fear itself

as we swallow the earth
it shall swallow us whole
we eat and are eaten
we die and depart
wise man   fool   **Arcturian**
WE ALL SHALL FALL FROM GRACE

some say you were a wise man
others that you were a fool

yesterday I saw you scattering
starflowers in the open skies

as you have faltered -

so shall you rise again

Bard of The South

words shall not be hid
nor spells buried
might shall not sink underground
though the mighty go
kalevala

bard of the south bard of twilight
you oversing your songs of love
poetize   romanticize
upon your *kantele* lamenting

angling for tears in lovers' eyes
missing truth that before you lies
life is simple   death is final
don't you see - **love is there at hand**

you see not what the future brings
nor where days of the past have gone
immersed in your soliloquy
- blinkered to the light of the sun

you see no more than any man
who breathes and walks upon this earth
indeed you see far less than most
so why pretend that you know more

you are greater than no other
and no lesser than no other
your love does not transcend your time
your life is worth no more than mine

it's **you** must change the course of fate
no-one else can do it for you
- what point is there to creating
beyond the joy in creation

*who needs a **trans-eternal love***
uniting distant spheres of time
- you only need to hear a voice
speak over the telephone line

who can determine the future
islands unknown beyond our sight
- live until your life-breath expires

surrender your love to the stars

<u>Sun in Our Eyes</u>

```
I think        I see              a sun
   I dream        I walk the clouds
    I begin to feel your warmth
     I seem to float on high


        of a sudden
        the door is flung
    wide                    open
    light ineffable  world on fire
  all I believed before was illusion
 all I had seen was the veil of maya
```

I know that we never exist alone
You are with us wherever we are
I know I am also **Apeiron**
the unlimited the unbounded

I know we all are starborn people
I know we were moulded from clay of gold
I know that I am **you** *and* **me**
my father and mother   my sister and lover

POESIA NUEVA

I know it was fear that restrained me
I know that we cannot survive without love
was ever a soul more famished and weak
than the one that survived without love

I know I embrace your love in my heart
and can capture your thoughts in my hand
I know that mind is just clouded emotion
and logos a source of delusion

*I know that **God** I create in my mind*
"You did not exist before"
the gates of heaven and hell   I make
tell me   **whose is divine law**

I know that time is in these skies
and space is in our minds
and earth   the land of tranquil light
rotates in the Indigo Blue

THE SUN IS IN OUR EYES, BUT ALL WE SEE IS RAIN
THE FIRE BURNS IN OUR HEARTS
BUT WE DON'T FEEL THE FLAME
THE SUN IS IN OUR EYES, BUT WE DON'T SEE IT SHINE
THE JOY IS RIGHT BEFORE US
*- **ALL WE FEEL IS PAIN***

<u>SAT CHIT ANANDA</u>

losing my time in the house of the blind
I did not know which way to go

"take me away   I cannot stay
- show me the light of day"

I would taste of the love bliss eternal
walk the SADHANA to SAT CHIT ANANDA

mind seeking union   life seeking love
I want to become as a part of you all

I want to surrender my self to my Self
I am ready for Your intoxication

ready to leave the cloud of unknowing
to slip with this body in unconscious depths

I would taste of the love bliss eternal
walk the SADHANA to SAT CHIT ANANDA

a geometry of emotions unfound
nor logic of feeling   nor algebra of love

*"would you taste of the love bliss eternal
walk the S*ADHANA *to S*AT *C*HIT *A*NANDA

*the pathway to love is always open
welcome   enter this house today*

*ask and you will be told what to do
- act and it will be given to you*

*no-one can know more love than
you it is yours as much as mine*

*love bliss eternal is here in the
present the future and yesterday*

*walk the S*ADHANA *to S*AT *C*HIT *A*NANDA

open your heart today"

Edouard d'Araille

In a Short Space of Time

I hear you breathe unsleeping
          in the unquiet grave of night
I meet you walk unthinking
          in that deathful house
             deprived of sight

do not wait an instant longer
    dispel the darkness
    part this day -
      leave this mansion
          far behind
    and enter empires of supernal light

it's where you are
        it's where you've always been
in here in time
          out there in space
unfound in body
          in matter encased
it's where you are
        to here you always shall return
though you may leave
      as soon as you
    in a short space of time   *awake*

the narcissist is nailed to the mirror -
                              words unsenseless
writing in the broken glass
"what was imagined and what was unreal
why say with eyes
what your open mouth conceals"

God only knows what God only knows
I do not want to have the love you cannot give
believe only in words of the body
                              in poetry of the flesh
believing only the glint in your eye
                              do not believe they lie

walking into our waking dreams
                swimming unrestless stolen streams
flesh rejuvenating flesh
                minds reopening folds in time
figures pacing passageways
                transfigured by light
                              of source unseen

with setting moon at amber dawn -
will we return in a short space of time
- to where we are, to where we've always been

"Even We Are In Arcadia"

since you are destined to return
depart with a tranquil mind
seneca

even we are in **Arcadia**
treading dew-soaked grass at dawn
summer sun   a frozen landscape
moon-cloud gleaming   willow trees

standing on the borderland
I was there but I did not see
there I met Thee wandering
- there you spoke these words to me

"I am birth and death and
I am youth and old age alike
I trace the cycles of time with
this scythe
I furrow the fields of life with
this plough

you are neither young nor agèd
neither here nor nowhere
you cross the frontier every night
from the transient into the ageless

a clock that has no minute hand
a clock that chimes no hours
a clock that does not measure time
a clock that shall not stop

each passing day advance
one day toward your birth
each passing day step one day
further from your death!"

why do our minds remain unopened
- the truth is forever disclosed
*even **we** are in **Arcadia***
sun in our eyes and song in our ears

whose the closest union of intimacy
whose not pleasure but bliss and joy
why love the other that you are
except that it is you yourself

"you are the river of Being itself
your body the gates of the Cosmos
you do not need to look any further
you seek what you hide from yourself"

EVEN WE ARE IN ARCADIA
we shall always come back here
EVEN WE ARE IN ARCADIA
a haven in space   at peace in time

EVEN WE ARE IN ARCADIA
entranced by the marble dusk
the cloud of apprehension passed
the broken road of time now crossed

EVEN WE ARE IN ARCADIA
treading dew-soaked grass at dawn
summer sun   a frozen landscape
moon-cloud gleaming   willow trees

- and when the time comes
this scene to be left   an hour
that may come soon   sleep well
sweet dreams   see pictures of
your loved one as you sleep

7. MISCELLANEOUS

(1997-2001)

I AM IN THE CAVE AGAIN

PLATON - TU AVAIS RAISON !

[Selections of verse from
over the years, representing
a variety of different styles
and interests; works that do
not as easily find a place in
other published collections]

<u>JEAN-LOUIS d'ARAGON</u>

Jean-Louis d'Aragon

you are neither

noble rich

nor grand.

Your house

is on this earth.

Your castle is not

in the vault of the skies.

I thought that I knew you

a moment but you were

a phantom   a ghost

from out of the past.

I thought that you were royal,

I found out that all

that you were

was soiled by lies

- *even your name*

is not your own -

"Jean Argand" you prefer

the **d** though you

were not aristocracy,

but only the king

of the alleys who

lives where he lays

his hat and stick and coat.

Edouard d'Araille

<u>Scotch on the Rocks</u>

the early morning
whisky drinkers are
always here at an hour the same

you cannot stop
them drinking no
more than halt a train on its tracks

every day they take the same:

"scotch on the rocks
with a double twist"

that was the drink that
they first drank when they
met in the café of the sun

they drink a dozen and
then they are ready
to take on the world again

WISDOM WITH AGE

children

screaming

running fast

ball escaped

game   lost

cronies

gossiping

distant past

cigar   club

incendiary

ashes dust

<u>*NOUVEAU RIMBAUD*</u>

"Le soleil a noirci la flamme des bougies;
Ainsi, toujours vainqueur, ton fantôme est pareil,
Ame resplendissante, à l'immortel soleil!"
CHARLES BAUDELAIRE

Out of the Unfeeling Void,
Out of the Absence
of Life and Love
comes you - **You**,
the Ineffable Soul
that no word could
ever describe   or name.

Out of the depths of Hell
you arose
                    from the
heights of the sky you fell.

- the Sun could not burn
your wings
and the earth could not
bind your legs.

POESIA **NUEVA**

You arrived
and the winds
that announced
the new tide swept
aside the dreams of a
hundred, thousand men
who had not yet lived or seen.

And they read and they ask
several centuries hence :

"Are you the Soul of my soul?
are you Pillar upon which
the Earth does rest?
I cannot believe
in this book,
- a man,
are you that?
or an angel or beast?'

Tell me the "Truth"
is true
and tell me the lies are not
UN-true.

I had not foreseen the future
but you had predicted the past.
Take me back from
whence I came -
I am not the stuff
such as souls are made of.
I am not the traveller
who wanders afar,
Time is too long and
the Earth is too wide."

A line has underscored the time

____

we lived, - and now that is gone,

what is a player without a scene,
- and what is an earth
without a sun?

What is a rabbit
without a hole and
a drunk without his dive?

POESIA NUEVA

Eternal Bard, - you sing
for too long, *and what
is the point of your song?*

You search for the
shapes of the *ABSOLUTE*
yet all that you see
is your wine-stained hand, -
You are poisoned by your words
and your life is intoxicated
with '*LOVE SUPREME*'.

What is the point
of destroying what you will
desire created - *again at dawn?*

Will there some day
be a Nouveau Rimbaud
- a sapling that talks
like an Ageless Oak?
Will he tell us again
the truth we ignore
in versified stanzas
with *nouveau absinthe :*

Edouard d'Araille

"We dream of a world
that is incomplete and
the death we foresee
it is not the end,
one part, only one,
of a life far more long,
who says God will not laugh
when the drama is done?

What is the nature
of "Inspiration", -

To capture the Heart
of a moment in Time?

I watch the flight
of a petal that falls
like a tear from a rose
as we follow the hearse."

HELLO MR. NEUTRON BOMB

hello Mr. Neutron Bomb!
you kept me waiting long

hello Mr. Neutron Bomb!
you said you'd be along

did it have a reason
tell me
was it all for fun?

hello Mr. Neutron Bomb,

thank God you came along!

<u>The House in Chelsea</u>

*"Well they must be wealthy,
they live in Chelsea! -
Their door is enormous.
Their credit is healthy.*

*Their settee is leather,
their wardrobe is velvet
- cocktails for breakfast
and 'bifteque' for tea.*

*I have not met them
but one day hope to,
await introductions,
to join "the club" -*

*If the parakeet answers
'GOOD MOURNING, SAR!'
they say
that is an omen
that paves the stair."*

My eels and mash have
gone cold with my thinking,
oh well, maybe the liquor
can heat them up;

I turn to my wife who
has told me the stories
and think to myself 'mid
the clatter and screams:

"Why can't we be wealthy
and live in Chelsea?
- Why do we live in
the gutter South-East?

Why can't we have grapes
and a crystal decanter
on a table veneered
in a burgundy lounge?"

As I knock back my tea
that is curdled and green,
I dream words in my ears
- '*GOOD MOURNING, SAR!*'

A Prologue

I am Starting
at the beginning -
though I do not know
where it really begins.

I only remember things
vaguely now - I cannot
recall them clear.

Out of the Fire

I leapt - I awoke,
there in the body
of man - *once more!*

Above the horizon
the eye of the Sun,
beneath my feet
- the Ground.

Some of You here
were beside me
then and a mother
and father I had like You.

As from an infant I turned
into man -
to the world
You opened a door Beyond.

Although I had joined
You long before
You had not
noticed me
in your midst.

Years I passed
in your
sleeping death -

You did not see Me pass.

Edouard d'Araille

In an indiscernible
darkness
lost,
not a
single sky
star could I kiss.

I did not even know
my face -
and nor
did you know my name.

Of a sudden a light
had unclosed
my eyes
around mc
all scapes of land gone

- now the earth has
no edges,
now
all is formless,
undivided,
one.

POESIA <u>NUEVA</u>

I spend the days
in carving
sculptures
of others whom I know;

yet they know not
the figures they see
for they recognize
not themselves!

They look to me
like fishes -
swimming
- the river
they do not see,

*I THOUGHT
I WOULD NEVER AWAKE
LIKE THEM.*

**I THOUGHT
I WOULD NEVER AWAKE !**

12/09/2001

CAN'T WE AWAKEN

    MUST WE FOREVER DEAR FRIENDS

        DIE IN OUR SLEEP?

CHARLES BUKOWSKI

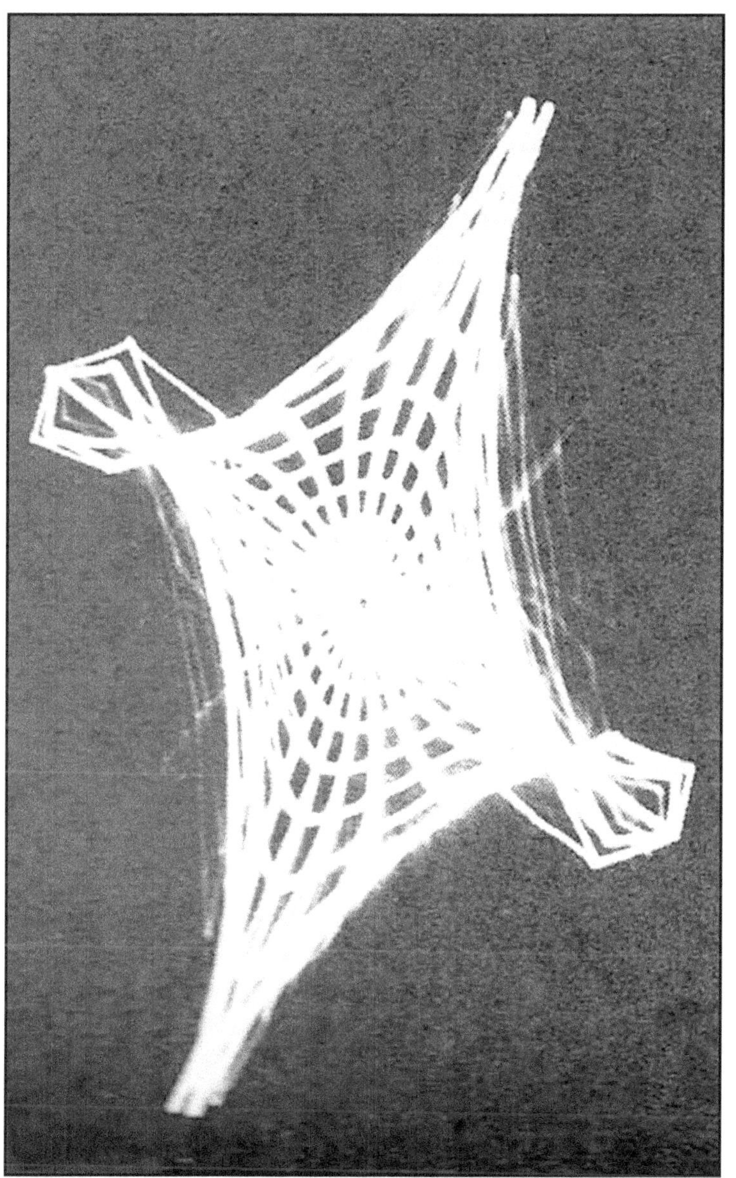